Acting Edition

Marie and Rosetta

by George Brant

‖SAMUEL FRENCH‖

Copyright © 2017 by George Brant
All Rights Reserved

MARIE AND ROSETTA is fully protected under the copyright laws of the United States of America, the British Commonwealth, including Canada, and all member countries of the Berne Convention for the Protection of Literary and Artistic Works, the Universal Copyright Convention, and/or the World Trade Organization conforming to the Agreement on Trade Related Aspects of Intellectual Property Rights. All rights, including professional and amateur stage productions, recitation, lecturing, public reading, motion picture, radio broadcasting, television, online/digital production, and the rights of translation into foreign languages are strictly reserved.

ISBN 978-0-573-70641-7

www.concordtheatricals.com
www.concordtheatricals.co.uk

FOR PRODUCTION INQUIRIES

UNITED STATES AND CANADA
info@concordtheatricals.com
1-866-979-0447

UNITED KINGDOM AND EUROPE
licensing@concordtheatricals.co.uk
020-7054-7298

Each title is subject to availability from Concord Theatricals Corp., depending upon country of performance. Please be aware that *MARIE AND ROSETTA* may not be licensed by Concord Theatricals Corp. in your territory. Professional and amateur producers should contact the nearest Concord Theatricals Corp. office or licensing partner to verify availability.

CAUTION: Professional and amateur producers are hereby warned that *MARIE AND ROSETTA* is subject to a licensing fee. The purchase, renting, lending or use of this book does not constitute a license to perform this title(s), which license must be obtained from Concord Theatricals Corp. prior to any performance. Performance of this title(s) without a license is a violation of federal law and may subject the producer and/or presenter of such performances to civil penalties. Both amateurs and professionals considering a production are strongly advised to apply to the appropriate agent before starting rehearsals, advertising, or booking a theatre. A licensing fee must be paid whether the title(s) is presented for charity or gain and whether or not admission is charged. Professional/Stock licensing fees are quoted upon application to Concord Theatricals Corp.

This work is published by Samuel French, an imprint of Concord Theatricals Corp.

No one shall make any changes in this title(s) for the purpose of production. No part of this book may be reproduced, stored in a retrieval system, scanned, uploaded, or transmitted in any form, by any means, now known or yet to be invented, including mechanical, electronic, digital, photocopying, recording, videotaping, or otherwise, without the prior written permission of the publisher. No one shall share this title(s), or any part of this title(s), through any social media or file hosting websites.

For all inquiries regarding motion picture, television, online/digital and other media rights, please contact Concord Theatricals Corp.

MUSIC AND THIRD-PARTY MATERIALS USE NOTE

Licensees are solely responsible for obtaining formal written permission from copyright owners to use copyrighted music and/or other copyrighted third-party materials (e.g. artworks, logos) in the performance of this play and are strongly cautioned to do so. If no such permission is obtained by the licensee, then the licensee must use only original music and materials that the licensee owns and controls. Licensees are solely responsible and liable for clearances of all third-party copyrighted materials, including without limitation music, and shall indemnify the copyright owners of the play(s) and their licensing agent, Concord Theatricals Corp., against any costs, expenses, losses and liabilities arising from the use of such copyrighted third-party materials by licensees. For music, please contact the appropriate music licensing authority in your territory for the rights to any incidental music.

IMPORTANT BILLING AND CREDIT REQUIREMENTS

If you have obtained performance rights to this title, please refer to your licensing agreement for important billing and credit requirements.

MARIE AND ROSETTA had its world premiere presented by the Atlantic Theatre Company in New York City on September 14, 2016. The performance was directed by Neil Pepe, with scenic design by Riccardo Hernández, costume design by Dede M. Ayite, lighting design by Christopher Akerlind, and sound design by Sck Sound Design. The pianist was Deah Love and the guitarist was Felicia M. Collins. The Production Stage Manager was Michael Domue. The cast was as follows:

SISTER ROSETTA THARPE .... Kecia Lewis
MARIE KNIGHT .... Rebecca Naomi Jones

MARIE AND ROSETTA was developed at TheatreWorks Silicon Valley as part of their New Works Festival. Additional development at The Playwrights' Center and The New Harmony Project.

CHARACTERS

SISTER ROSETTA THARPE – An African-American woman in her early thirties. Pretty, vivacious, an irrepressible spirit. A mean guitar player with a bluesy voice. Sings spirituals that swing.

MARIE KNIGHT – An African-American woman in her early twenties, but looks younger. A more traditional alto gospel singer, plays staid piano at first. Gorgeous, on her way to being a spiritual star.

SETTING

Mississippi, 1946

AUTHOR'S NOTES

A note about ages: in historical reality, Sister Rosetta was in her early thirties and Marie in her early twenties in 1946. Productions are welcome to adjust these ages as needed for casting purposes, as long as an age gap of some kind between the two actors is preserved. Their relationship may have more of a sisterly or maternal edge as a result of the actors' ages, but should avoid feeling predatory in any way.

Musicians

If the actors playing Marie and Rosetta are not virtuoso guitarists/pianists, their instruments may be "voiced" by professional musicians. These musicians should also be African-American females.

Sincere and heartfelt thanks to all who supported, encouraged, and lifted up this play in its journey
(in order of appearance)

Laura Kepley, Sam Phillips, Gayle Wald, Anthony Heilbut, The Playwrights' Center, Jeremy Cohen, Wendy Knox, Cristiana Clark, Dominic Taylor, Mat Smart, Sanford Moore, The Gersh Agency, Jessica Amato, Ivory Doublette, ShaVunda Horsley, Kate Navin, The New Harmony Project, Mead Hunter, Joel Grynheim, Team Joy, Erica Nagel, Josh Kight, Danielle Brooks, Chaz Hodges, Anna Rhoads, TheatreWorks Silicon Valley, Giovanna Sardelli, Robert Kelley, Michelle E. Jordan, William Liberatore, Scott Rudin, The Atlantic Theater, Neil Pepe, Jeffory Lawson, Annie MacRae, Rebecca Naomi Jones, Kecia Lewis, Felicia M. Collins, Deah Harriott, Steve Broadnax, Jason Michael Webb, Michael Domue, Abigail Katz, Seth Glewen, and Mark Carpentieri.

For the incomparable Sister Rosetta Tharpe and Madame Marie Knight

(1946, Mississippi. A showroom in a modest funeral home. Several coffins, folding chairs, a spinet piano. Out of place are several open suitcases on the floor and propped up on chairs, a number of guitar cases, and a few dresses hung up on open coffin lids.)

(Two women dressed in formal gowns sit facing each other on folding chairs: **MARIE**, *a beautiful, radiant woman who looks about eighteen, and* **ROSETTA**, *a pretty, vivacious, plump woman in her early thirties.* **MARIE** *is putting the final touches on* **ROSETTA**'s *makeup, humming "Peace in the Valley."* **ROSETTA**'s *eyes are closed.)*

*(***MARIE*** steps back, evaluates her handiwork, hopes it's good enough. She girds herself, and:)*

MARIE. Miss Tharpe?

   Miss Tharpe?

ROSETTA. *(Eyes still closed, correcting.)* Sister

MARIE. Sister

   I think I'm done

ROSETTA. *(Still closed.)* Hm?

MARIE. Everything but the lips just like you said

ROSETTA. Lips?

MARIE. Everything but

   Just like you said

ROSETTA. Right

      *(***ROSETTA*** opens her eyes.)*

Mercy

I musta fell asleep

You gotta gentle touch

MARIE. Gentle
Scared

ROSETTA. Of what

MARIE. Of messing up
Not sure how much is too much yet
How much blush you need to survive that spotlight

ROSETTA. Shoot
Blush ain't armor girl
Blush just brings what's on the inside out
How 'bout my scar?

MARIE. What scar?

ROSETTA. Listen to you
You know what scar
You had to see my scar my forehead staring right at you
You cover it up?

MARIE. Yes ma'am

ROSETTA. *Sister*
Well then let's see
Mirror

MARIE. Oh
Maybe I

(MARIE touches ROSETTA up.)

ROSETTA. You said you were done girl

MARIE. I know but

ROSETTA. Mirror

(MARIE acquiesces, hands ROSETTA a mirror, steps back. ROSETTA examines MARIE's handiwork silently. A moment as MARIE braces for the worst.)

MARIE. Is it

ROSETTA. Dear God

MARIE. I'm sorry I

ROSETTA. Dear sweet Jesus
MARIE. If you let me just
ROSETTA. Sister ain't never looked better
MARIE. I could put more – what?
ROSETTA. You got the cheeks
Nobody gets the cheeks
You got the cheeks real good
MARIE. You think so? Really?
ROSETTA. And they the most important part
When I look up to Heaven
People gotta see Heaven looking down
Shining on my big ole cheeks
Blessing them
Ooo they blessed now they most surely are blessed
Like a couple'a halos on my face
MARIE. I'm glad real glad
ROSETTA. I saw it I knew I saw it
It wasn't just your singin'
I swear there was a light
There was some kinda light over your head last night and I knew I had to either ignore that light to pretend I didn't see nothing or to let that light into my heart and find out what God had planned for it
And look what He had planned
He had these cheeks in His plan
MARIE. *(Blushing.)* The lips should I
ROSETTA. *(Teasing.)* Lips lips
What you in such a hurry to get to my lips for?
MARIE. *(Deer in the headlights.)* Oh no I'm not I
ROSETTA. You got plans for them little girl?
MARIE. No I
ROSETTA. Well ain't that a shame
MARIE. I don't I
ROSETTA. Lord awful easy to make you blush little girl

    Don't even need me a brush
MARIE. Sorry Miss Tharpe
ROSETTA. *Sister*
    And relax
    I ain't worried 'bout lips
    Lips're easy anybody can do lips
    Lips are a kiss
    Can't do 'em yet anyway
    We got singin' to do first

        (Returning to the mirror.)

    Dear Jesus would you look at your Rosetta
    I swear every man in my hand just got fired
    They just got the pink slip every one
MARIE. Because of blush?
ROSETTA. You think Kermit can put on blush?
    With his big ole ugly drummer hands?
    I shoulda found me a gal sooner
    Pink slips for all'a 'em every one

        (They laugh for a moment, then:)

    You ain't said nothin' 'bout yours
MARIE. Mine?
ROSETTA. Your face
MARIE. Oh I thought I I'm sure I did
ROSETTA. Nope
MARIE. Oh well I think it's
ROSETTA. Too late now you said it all
MARIE. No no I love it it's
ROSETTA. That was your cue see
    You gonna have to learn to pick up your cues
    That's all this is gonna be you know
    You and me
    Pickin' up cues
MARIE. I know and I'm so
ROSETTA. So pick it up

MARIE. I love it
ROSETTA. Like you mean it
MARIE. It's perfect
ROSETTA. Without skipping a beat
MARIE. Like I got two little halos sitting on my cheeks
ROSETTA. Yeah
Yeah
Yeah you do look mighty good don't you
Ooo-ooo!
Look at that
I had a little part in that
Feel like I should sign it somewhere
That face of yours
In the corner on the jawline or something
MARIE. *(Blushing.)* Now
ROSETTA. No you can blush all you want but between me and Jesus we made us a masterpiece
MARIE. *(Blushing.)* Thank you

>*(**ROSETTA** moves to the piano.)*

ROSETTA. Now let's make a little Good News in here

>*(**ROSETTA** plays a phrase on the piano.)*

Poster says we got a show tonight

[MUSIC NO. 00 "ROSETTA AT THE PIANO"]

Better come up with one
MARIE. We're rehearsing here?
ROSETTA. There a piano on the bus?
MARIE. No
But this place

>*(The funeral home.)*

My goosebumps got goosebumps
ROSETTA. This?
Oh you better tell them goosebumps to settle down honey

We here for the duration

MARIE. The duration?

No

The show isn't here

ROSETTA. No

MARIE. So we rehearse a little here and then we're gone

ROSETTA. Yep

But then we back

MARIE. Back?

ROSETTA. That's right

Where you think we sleep?

MARIE. Sleep?

(Horrible truth dawning.)

No

ROSETTA. We not in New York anymore honey

MARIE. No no

ROSETTA. We not in Chicago

MARIE. No

ROSETTA. Can't stay in no hotel down here

MARIE. But you

You're famous

ROSETTA. To some folk

To the thousand or so Leroys and Wandalyns coming tonight

To the rest of Mississippi I'm just another nigger

MARIE. You?

ROSETTA. Why you think we got a white bus driver?

Who else gonna buy us food?

Who else gonna talk to those flashing lights if we get pulled over?

When we get pulled over?

MARIE. You're serious

ROSETTA. Honey

Maybe you noticed

We ain't playin' no Carnegie Hall tonight
No Savoy Ballroom
No Café Society
We playin' in a warehouse
Tobacco warehouse on the outskirts of town
Dresses gonna stink of smoke for a week
Next night's a barn
After that a hangar
Anywhere a bunch a black folk congregatin' won't be noticed
There's rules down here
We northern Negroes
We got to be invisible
We step off stage and we got to disappear
And beds?
Down here we depend on the Good Samaritan Circuit for a bed cuz God knows there ain't no room at the inn
Sometimes it's somebody's garage
Kitchen
Couch
And sometimes it's a miracle like this
A piano in the corner
Plenty a' elbow space
And a showroom to choose from for when we lay down our heads

MARIE. Lay down – where –?

ROSETTA. Your choice
Cot or casket

MARIE. You can't be –

ROSETTA. I'm a casket gal myself
Like sleeping on a cloud

MARIE. I could never

ROSETTA. Suit yourself
Cot it is

MARIE. Not even a cot
  Not here
  I won't be able to sleep
  All night looking for ghosts
ROSETTA. Well you keep an eye out for ghosts I'm gonna be snoring in the corner
  In the deluxe satin-lined model
  And you thank Walter in the morning you hear?
  Whether you sleep all night or just a minute cuz'a ghost-watchin' you thank him
  Good Samaritan Walter of "Walter's Funeral Home and Insurance Company"
  Cuz without him little Marie would be sleeping the night in the bus cute little black girl out there sleeping under her coat pretty face in the window for all the white world to see
MARIE. All right
  I'll thank him
ROSETTA. Who?
MARIE. Walter
ROSETTA. Good
  Someday I'll get enough money
  Deck that bus out put some beds in there
  Mirrors closets dressing rooms
  Won't have to worry 'bout this every night
  Until then we depend on our friends
  Wherever we find them
  Understood?
MARIE. Understood
ROSETTA. It's not all funeral parlors honey
MARIE. All right
ROSETTA. But it's more than one
  Nothing to be scared of though
  Nothing but a bunch of souls gone to Glory
MARIE. But don't rehearsing here seem a little

Like
Like maybe we're not respecting them enough

ROSETTA. Respecting them?
No
They like the music

(**ROSETTA** *jauntily underscores the following.*)

Better than that sad old organ wheezing through they service
We give 'em something good before they move on
Something to remember
Something to tap their tootsies to on their way to the pearly gates

(Piano out.)

MARIE. You're joking with me

ROSETTA. A little
It's awful easy
You ever joke?
Or you serious all the time
Makeup is one thing
Singing
But are you gonna be any fun?

MARIE. I'm fun
I think
Plenty fun

ROSETTA. Well give me some warning or I may have a heart attack
Raise your hand or something 'fore you tell a joke
So I know it's comin'

MARIE. I will

ROSETTA. That was a joke

MARIE. I know

ROSETTA. Ooo-eee fish in a barrel

MARIE. I guess I don't
Don't get too much practice

Mama's not too fond of fun
Says no joke in the Bible
Not one
Says if the Lord meant for us to have fun He'd'a put at least one in there

ROSETTA. That true?
There's gotta be a joke or two

MARIE. Nope

ROSETTA. If you say so
But there's joy right?

MARIE. There's joy

ROSETTA. Damn right –

(To MARIE.)

Pardon

(To Heaven.)

Pardon
– There's joy
It's all Joy is what it is
The whole Book
Right
Whether it's suffering or celebration
It's all about Joy

MARIE. Yes but

ROSETTA. Well maybe you found different in your many years on this earth but me I found where there's Joy there's a joke

MARIE. Guess so

ROSETTA. That's what Mahalia and all them don't understand
Saint Mahalia
God ain't up there frownin' down on all'a us
Shakin' his head
His Holy finger
Pursin' his lips every time we cross some imaginary line

No
God up there chucklin' away at all'a us
All us saints and sinners
Can't wait to see what his silly children gonna come up with next

MARIE. But Mama

ROSETTA. No disrespect to your mama
No disrespect but we got to have us some fun
We got to have us some fun or your mama can have you right back again

MARIE. Yes ma'am

ROSETTA. Sister Sister
Tell you what
We'll give this tonight
You and me
See how it goes
Tonight and we'll see where we at

MARIE. Tonight

ROSETTA. Now let's go
We got a show to put together
My fans are comin' whether we ready or not
'Bout now Leroy's out there slappin' on aftershave and Wandalyn's done picking out her dress

(**ROSETTA** *starts to launch into a song on the piano, interrupted by:*)

MARIE. 'Course but could I –?
Could I hear you alone first?
Just to get used to you
You right in front of me like this so close

ROSETTA. You stallin'

MARIE. No it's only

ROSETTA. My world ain't no time for stallin'

MARIE. Please
Just one song

ROSETTA. All right
But no more stallin' after
Little girl got a request?

MARIE. I love "Strange Things"
'Bout wore that one out

ROSETTA. Mmm I'm not feeling that one yet gotta warm up to that one that's the closer
Oh
I got something
Lay down the ground rules for you

>*(**ROSETTA** launches into the next song, her piano playing with an unexpected amount of swing for a gospel song, and her singing somehow both full of devotion and mischief.)*

[MUSIC NO. 01 "THIS TRAIN"]

THIS TRAIN IS A CLEAN TRAIN, THIS TRAIN
THIS TRAIN IS A CLEAN TRAIN, THIS TRAIN
THIS TRAIN IS A CLEAN TRAIN
EVERYBODY RIDIN' IT IN JESUS' NAME
THIS TRAIN IS A CLEAN TRAIN, THIS TRAIN

THIS TRAIN DON'T PULL NO LIARS, THIS TRAIN
THIS TRAIN DON'T PULL NO LIARS, THIS TRAIN
THIS TRAIN DON'T PULL NO LIARS
NO HYPOCRITES AND NO HIGH FLYERS
THIS TRAIN DON'T PULL NO LIARS, THIS TRAIN

THIS TRAIN IS BOUND FOR GLORY, THIS TRAIN
THIS TRAIN IS BOUND FOR GLORY, THIS TRAIN
THIS TRAIN IS BOUND FOR GLORY
DON'T RIDE NOTHIN' BUT THE RIGHTEOUS AND THE HOLY
THIS TRAIN IS BOUND FOR GLORY, THIS TRAIN!

>*(**ROSETTA** wraps it up. **MARIE** is overwhelmed.)*

MARIE. Oh my

ROSETTA. No no that was just okay I haven't warmed up yet

MARIE. No

No
It was more than okay
Oh my

> (**MARIE** *is almost hyperventilating.*)

ROSETTA. Keep breathin' girl

MARIE. It's just
It's
It's a lot –

ROSETTA. A lotta what?

MARIE. For one day
It's a lot that's all
Time always moves so fast for me but this must be some kind of record
One day ago you were a face on an album cover
A voice in my bedroom
Someone to sing along with when I was feeling low-down
And now you're here
In front of me
Singing "This Train"
Telling me I'm good with blush
It's a lot

ROSETTA. Just keep breathin'

MARIE. Last night I was an opening act
A voice in a quartet
I wasn't even standing in the middle
I was off to the side
The left-hand side
End of the line
And now
One day later
I don't
Why just me?

ROSETTA. Huh?

MARIE. Why didn't you take all of us?
ROSETTA. I didn't need all of you
MARIE. But we sounded good right?
ROSETTA. *You* sounded good
MARIE. But I shouldn't've
That means I stuck out
How'd I stick out
It's quartet singing
I'm not supposed to stick out
ROSETTA. Honey you?
You'd stick out anywhere
MARIE. But I
ROSETTA. 'Sides
Those other three sounded tight
Nervous
No wonder
Openin' up for Saint Mahalia
The next big thing
Make anybody nervous
But not you
MARIE. Trembling my hands were trembling
ROSETTA. But your voice wasn't
That voice of yours
I saw Mahalia watching you from the wings
I know her well enough she was gonna snatch you up for herself if I didn't grab you first
MARIE. That's what Mama said
Said she was bound to come calling
ROSETTA. Your mama's smart
I knew I had to move
And you lucky I did
Mahalia woulda stuck you in her choir just one more voice in that choir that's what I told your mama
MARIE. You did?

ROSETTA. Last night at our little midnight summit
>Our little post-show pow-wow in your folks' front parlor
>I'm sitting there contract in my hand
>Bus idling outside ready to take us away
>But your mama
>Your mama wanted to hold out for Mahalia
>I could tell
>She wanted to wait till the Saint came marchin' in
>But I told your mama
>And it was truth
>Mahalia woulda wasted you on those heavenly "ooo's" and "ahh's" while she did her business up front
>Me
>I ain't gonna waste you
>You see a choir?

MARIE. No

ROSETTA. I told your mama
>Me?
>I'm gonna let your little light shine
>You good with that?

MARIE. Good

ROSETTA. And playing piano?

MARIE. Piano?

ROSETTA. You'll be the one on piano
>I heard you last night
>I know you're better than me

MARIE. No

ROSETTA. I can plunk around but

MARIE. You sounded wonderful

ROSETTA. Not as good as you do though

MARIE. Well
>Of course you –

ROSETTA. Don't lie to me girl

We can't build this up on no lyin' foundation
You tell the truth or we over before we start
Who's better on piano?
Huh?

>   *(**MARIE** struggles, but finally answers honestly.)*

MARIE. Me
ROSETTA. That's right you
You better
You own up to your gifts girl
You got to know what they worth
Truly worth
Or you got nothing
My Mother Bell taught me that
I was little girl eight or so
Mother Bell and I step out to sing middle of the service
I'm all decked out in a new dress and hat
Black folk in front of me smiling and praising
And then I look up
See all them white folk in the balcony
Up in the Heaven section
The ones who showed up every Sunday for a little entertainment
Come to see the holy rollers in action
And then I hear it
A distant sound
A jingle jangle in pockets
I see a glint of something and feel a sting on my cheek
And then the shower proper starts
The copper shower from the balcony
Pennies from Heaven
And some of the black folk are scrambling to pick 'em up but I know Mother Bell told me not to lower myself not to be one of those scramblers but my cheek stings it was kissed by one of them and I

know what a penny buys just one how much candy that one penny buys and I see it at my feet it's there at my feet the one that kissed me and I slide my right foot over and cover that copper I'm thinking I'll save that one just that one and we finish and the clapping brings more copper but I don't pick them up I don't stoop I just shuffle I just shuffle-walk that penny back to the pew with my Mother Bell at my side and I'm thinkin' I finally outsmarted her for once but the minute we sit down she whacks that right leg of mine with her cane she didn't fall for my jake walk after all and now what do I got?

I got the eight-year-old blues:

A big ugly bruise on my leg and no penny to show for it

I was mad but Mother Bell was right

Even then

Even at eight years old I was worth more than a white man's pocket change

You got to know

You got to know what your gift's worth

MARIE. Yes Sister

    (**ROSETTA** *smiles guiltily.*)

ROSETTA. Shoot

As long as we're telling truth

Story had a happy ending

I'm standing around bored outta my mind at the coffee hour after the service

Smiling and nodding at all the old ladies who wanna pinch my cheek

And I 'scused myself

Got some punch in the corner

And I bent down to drink it

And something falls outta my hat

Plops right down into my punch

Kerplunk

And there it was

My own little fruit punch wishing well
And I looked around
No Mother Bell
And I figured I wasn't stooping
I wasn't scrambling around on the floor
I was just a proud little girl with a gift reaching into her punch cup and pulling out a prize
Wore a big ole hat the next week

    (MARIE and ROSETTA share a laugh.)

MARIE. I'll bet you did

ROSETTA. Six-inch brim
All right now
Let's hear it
Your gift now
Let's give those tremblin' hands somethin' to do

MARIE. What do you want to –?

ROSETTA. Surprise me

    (MARIE slowly sits at the piano, takes a deep breath to gather herself, and then plays a traditional, reverential version of "Were You There When They Crucified My Lord?" She starts a little hesitantly vocally, but by the end is in full and powerful contralto voice.)

[MUSIC NO. 02 "WERE YOU THERE"]

MARIE.
WERE YOU THERE WHEN THEY CRUCIFIED MY LORD?
WERE YOU THERE WHEN THEY CRUCIFIED MY LORD?
OH, SOMETIMES IT CAUSES ME TO TREMBLE, TREMBLE, TREMBLE
WERE YOU THERE WHEN THEY CRUCIFIED MY LORD?

WERE YOU THERE WHEN THEY LAID HIM IN THE TOMB?
WERE YOU THERE WHEN THEY LAID HIM IN THE TOMB?
OH, SOMETIMES IT CAUSES ME TO TREMBLE, TREMBLE, TREMBLE
WERE YOU THERE WHEN THEY LAID HIM IN THE TOMB?

> WERE YOU THERE WHEN HE A-ROSE UP FROM THE GRAVE?
> WERE YOU THERE WHEN HE ROSE UP FROM THE GRAVE?
> OH, SOMETIMES IT CAUSES ME TO TREMBLE, TREMBLE, TREMBLE
> WERE YOU THERE WHEN HE ROSE UP FROM THE GRAVE?
>
> (**MARIE** *finishes. There's a hush; the room has changed.*)

ROSETTA. Mercy
 Little girl got a little Mahalia in her

MARIE. I wasn't trying to copy

ROSETTA. I know you weren't
 You're more high church than me is all

MARIE. Is that bad?

ROSETTA. No little girl

> (*Correcting.*)

 Little *Sister*
 It could be perfect
 But first we gotta break you of a habit or two
 See if we can
 If it ain't too ingrained
 That vibrator natural?

MARIE. Pardon?

ROSETTA. Your vibrator?
 Natural?

MARIE. Oh!
 My vibrato?

ROSETTA. That's what I said

MARIE. No
 No not really

ROSETTA. Good
 I don't want to hear it
 Don't know why
 Never liked vibrator

Now how long you been singing?

MARIE. Long as I remember

ROSETTA. Soloing?

MARIE. Since I was nine

ROSETTA. And how 'bout the piano?

MARIE. Since 'bout six maybe

ROSETTA. Who taught you?

MARIE. Me

ROSETTA. Yeah
Me taught me too
Me's a good teacher
Sure gets around
Whose piano?

MARIE. Church's
I snuck in on off hours
Played while the janitor swept up
Put all those notes together one key at a time

ROSETTA. You wanted it

MARIE. I did

ROSETTA. You wanted it you knew it was something God gave you to share

MARIE. It made me happy

ROSETTA. That's right it's Good News that's what Good News is all about
Good
We might just be a good team

MARIE. A team?

ROSETTA. That's right

MARIE. But I'm not
You're a star
Millions of records
The biggest Gospel star there is

ROSETTA. Was
Saint Mahalia

MARIE. You're bigger than her
ROSETTA. For now
MARIE. You are
　She's big but
　Seems the world split down the middle
　People either Mahalia people or Rosetta people
ROSETTA. What're you?
MARIE. I'm a half-breed
ROSETTA. What?
MARIE. My mom's Mahalia my dad's you
　I gotta keep the peace
ROSETTA. I could tell your daddy was a Rosetta man
　Your mama did all the talkin' but I could tell your daddy had some swing in him
MARIE. He does he's fit to bust
ROSETTA. And your mama?
MARIE. She's fit for something
　Wouldn't stop praying over me
　Sending me out into the big wide world with you
　No chaperone
ROSETTA. Mmm
　'Bout that
　She made me promise lots of promises
MARIE. *(Embarrassed.)* Oh goodness no
ROSETTA. Made me promise to bring you back the way I found you
MARIE. Oh gosh she's so
ROSETTA. It's all right
　She cares about you
　That's a mama's job
　But

　　(Teasing, almost flirty.)
　If I'm gonna keep that promise...
MARIE. What?

ROSETTA. How did I find you?
MARIE. Pardon?
ROSETTA. If I'm bringing you back the same way...
MARIE. Oh
ROSETTA. What *way* am I bringing you back?
MARIE. ...I've kissed...a boy or two
ROSETTA. Prom?
MARIE. Mm-hm
ROSETTA. I wish I coulda seen that I bet you were a taffeta princess
MARIE. I don't know about that
ROSETTA. So that's it?
   A kiss or two?
MARIE. *(That's not it.)* Well...
ROSETTA. Now you got my attention
   Tell me
   What?
   You got a sweetheart?
MARIE. Sorta
ROSETTA. Sorta?
MARIE. I got a husband
ROSETTA. *(Knocked off-balance.)* Oh
   Musta married young
MARIE. Not really
ROSETTA. Oh
   I figured you for 'round seventeen
MARIE. Twenty-three
ROSETTA. Oh
MARIE. Is that –?
ROSETTA. Hold up
   Need to take a little stock
   Get all this right in my mind
   Twenty-three
MARIE. Uh-huh

ROSETTA. And a husband?

MARIE. Uh-huh

ROSETTA. Your mama was kinda playing up the pure little lamb thing
The innocent little girl
Keeping you out of the parlor while we decided your future
Like you wasn't an adult yourself

MARIE. Well
I mighta told her to

(The air becomes charged.)

ROSETTA. You?

MARIE. I thought that's what you wanted

ROSETTA. *You* thought?

MARIE. Why you wanted me
That you wanted someone who was a little more
A contrast

ROSETTA. Careful now
So
Twenty-three and a husband
Next thing you know you'll be telling me you got babies

(A moment.)

MARIE. Two

ROSETTA. Remind me not to play you in poker

MARIE. So
Was I right?
Is that why you want me?

ROSETTA. Truth
Yeah I want you for a contrast
But not just your look

MARIE. No?

ROSETTA. Your sound
That high church sound of yours

MARIE. What about it?

ROSETTA. Mixed with mine
    Might be just enough to get me back in the church folks' good graces
    I been in exile for too long
    Those gospel gates got locked behind me when I went out into the nightclubs
    Time for them to swing back open

MARIE. But you can't just expect people to
    Some of those songs you sang out there in the World
    You can't unsing them
    They're on record
    Forever

ROSETTA. So?

MARIE. They make people wonder
    Make me wonder

ROSETTA. Wonder what?

MARIE. If you're right
    Right with God

ROSETTA. You heard them records?

MARIE. I did

ROSETTA. They got joy?

MARIE. They do
    But I'm not sure it's the right kind

ROSETTA. There more than one kind?

MARIE. I think so
    Your joy…has hips

ROSETTA. Sure do
    And who made those hips
    Who made them swing

MARIE. I know
    I'm just
    I'm scared

ROSETTA. Of me?

MARIE. You're trying to get back in but I'm just starting out

This don't work
The two of us?
People still paint you with that sinful brush?
They're gonna paint me too
And I'll be over before I start
And more than that
I may have a husband
But I am pure
I am washed in the blood of the Lamb
I am sanctified
And I need to be brought back the way I was found

ROSETTA. I see
Well
God is my company-keeper too Little Sister don't you worry 'bout that none
I been forgiven for anything I've done
Jesus forgives me seven times seventy a day
You'll just have to believe
Faith
Think you can do that for tonight my little lamb?

(**MARIE** *nods, blushing.*)

There you go again
Blushing without blush
I don't think you as grown-up as you think
Now
Your piano
That's a different story
Your piano's a little *too* grown-up

MARIE. What?

ROSETTA. You better than me yeah but the way you play?
You gotta get your piano sounding a little younger girl
Your piano's an old maid with a grey tabby on her lap

MARIE. Now

ROSETTA. You need a little more barrelhouse in there a little more boogie

MARIE. You want high church
ROSETTA. In the voice that's all
Please
There's a limit
MARIE. But I can't
I can't swing like you
ROSETTA. Can't or won't?
MARIE. ...Little of both
ROSETTA. Thought so
Well
How 'bout we see if you "can" first and we'll worry about "won't" later
Now here

    (**ROSETTA** *grabs* **MARIE**'s *hips.*)

See if we can loosen these up
MARIE. Oh!
ROSETTA. Lord you stiff as a board
MARIE. I don't think
ROSETTA. Now swing
MARIE. I don't think they do
ROSETTA. Swing
MARIE. I
ROSETTA. Swing honey
Swing
Stop holding out on me Little Sister
They know how to swing
Two babies worth'a swing in those hips don't tell me different

    (**ROSETTA** *eventually gets a mortified* **MARIE**'s *hips to swing.*)

There you go
See you can
There it is
There

And then you just put this
> *(The hip swing.)*

Into this
> *(The piano.)*
>
> *(A flushed **MARIE** slinks to the piano bench.)*

Now let's see
What's a good one to practice on?

MARIE. How 'bout:

[MUSIC NO. 03 "AMAZING GRACE #1"]

> *(**MARIE** plays. **ROSETTA** cuts her off.)*

ROSETTA. No
  Lord
  One with hips
  Let's try "Rock Me"
  You need music?

MARIE. No I know most everything by heart

ROSETTA. Then go 'head

[MUSIC NO. 03A "BEFORE ROCK ME"]

> *(**MARIE** plays a few bars then stops, realizing it's too stiff.)*
>
> *(A moment.)*
>
> *(**MARIE** tries again: she eventually gains a touch of swing, but she stops abruptly.)*

Don't stop honey that's it

MARIE. It's not that
  It don't
  It don't feel right

> *(**ROSETTA** leans over **MARIE** to get to the keys.)*

ROSETTA. Honey
  There's this:

> *(**ROSETTA** plays a few bars straight.)*

ROSETTA. Or there's this:

> (**ROSETTA** *plays a few with swing.*)

Either way

(*Pointing to the Heavens.*) Those notes are all going to the same place

Some are just getting there with a little more style

Now try again

> (**MARIE** *nods, not entirely convinced, but tries again. She plays the intro to "Rock Me," still a little stiff, but it's getting there.*)

Better better

Here I come

[MUSIC NO. 04 "ROCK ME"]

> (**ROSETTA** *joins her, singing.*)

NOW WON'T YOU HEAR ME SWINGIN' –

> (**MARIE** *stops playing abruptly.*)

Why'd you –?

MARIE. (*Putting her foot down a bit.*) I'm sorry but it's "singing"

ROSETTA. What?

MARIE. The words

It's s'posed to be "singing" – "won't you hear me singing"
You sang "swinging"

ROSETTA. It's how I did it on the record

MARIE. I know

But that don't make it right

You took a gospel song and you made it sound...

ROSETTA. Go ahead

MARIE. ...Dirty

ROSETTA. Mr. Dorsey never complained

Million copies sold

Put a few more pennies in his pocket

MARIE. But you said yourself a few pennies can't be worth –
ROSETTA. What?
MARIE. The way you bend things around
　You don't worry about that?
　Your soul?
　There's a limit right?
　There has to be
ROSETTA. It's all praisin' Little Sister that's all
　"Praise Him with the sounding of the trumpet
　Praise Him with the harp and lyre"
　That's all we doin'
　Besides
　God don't want the Devil to have all the good music right?
MARIE. That's what Daddy'd say
ROSETTA. I like your daddy
MARIE. But I think I'd...
　I'd appreciate it if you'd sing it right
ROSETTA. Oh
　If I sang it "right"
　You'd appreciate it
MARIE. Long as I'm up there with you

　　(A stand-off, then:)

ROSETTA. All right Madame Marie
　I'll meet you partway
　You swinging for me I guess I can church it up for you
　But just so's you know Mr. Dorsey was a bluesman first
　Gospel born from the blues
　You think about that some all right?
　You think about that while we fight over a little hip
　Now from the top
　Old Wandalyn's slippin' on her wig

　　*(**MARIE** begins the song again. **ROSETTA** both sings and ad-libs, encouraging **MARIE**.)*

ROSETTA.
>NOW WON'T YOU HEAR ME SINGIN'
>HEAR THE WORDS THAT I'M SAYIN'
>WASH MY SOUL WITH WATER FROM ON HIGH
>WHILE THE WORLD OF LOVE IS AROUND ME
>EVIL THOUGHTS DO BIND ME
>BUT OH, IF YOU LEAVE ME
>I WILL DIE

>That's it girl

>YOU HOLD ME IN YOUR BOSOM
>TILL THE STORMS OF LIFE IS OVER
>RRRRRRRRRROCK ME

>>*(MARIE stops playing again, putting her foot down again, for real now.)*

MARIE. All right now that –!

ROSETTA. What now?

MARIE. That "Rock Me"
>You have to admit that sounds

ROSETTA. What do you want girl?
>A little more Mahalia?

>>*(Singing stiffly.)*

>ROCK ME IN THE CRADLE OF YOUR LOVE

>Now that's fine that's pretty
>But it don't sound like rockin' to me

MARIE. No
>But maybe your way sounds too much like rockin'

ROSETTA. *(Smiling.)* Maybe
>You didn't raise your hand

MARIE. What?

ROSETTA. To warn me
>That was awful close to a joke

MARIE. Yes but

ROSETTA. Now let's take it from "You hold –"

MARIE. Yes but would you maybe…?

ROSETTA. What?
MARIE. Less "rockin"?
ROSETTA. ...You serious
MARIE. I am

> (**ROSETTA** *is increasingly angry but trying to rein it in.*)

ROSETTA. My my my
  You must really be 'fraid of that sinful paint

> (**MARIE** *says nothing.*)

  From "You hold me"

> (**MARIE** *plays and a neutered* **ROSETTA** *sings.*)

YOU HOLD ME IN YOUR BOSOM
TILL THE STORMS OF LIFE IS OVER
ROCK ME
IN THE CRADLE OF OUR –

> (**ROSETTA** *throws up her hand, her turn to stop the proceedings. She turns on* **MARIE**.)

No!
No no no no no!
Who are *you*?
Some seventeen-year-old twenty-three-year-old come in here and think you can
No

> (*Defiantly, in* **MARIE**'s *face.*)

 RRRRRRROCK ME!
 RRRRRRROCK ME!
That's what the people down here come to see
That's what they travel on wagon ten miles to see
What they saved up for
What they dress up for
They come to hear that RRRRRROCK ME for theyselves
I am bringing them joy with that Rock Me you hear?
Joy

So no I ain't changin' that

And if you gonna be lookin' over my shoulder every second of every day then we can forget this whole thing right now

Why don't we do that why don't you stay here with your ghosts and I will rock that warehouse to the ground and tomorrow you can take your skinny ass –

(To **MARIE**.*)* Pardon

(To Heaven.) Pardon

– Back home

>   (**MARIE** *is chastened.*)

And as for your soul

Your precious pure two-baby soul

I'll take care of it as best I can but that

That's a personal thing

That's between you and the Lord

Me I know I'm right with Him you gotta fend for yourself

>   (**MARIE** *nods.*)

From "You hold me"

And honey?

That piano?

It's hip or the highway

>   (**MARIE** *nods and launches back into the song, doing her best now. Her playing does get more and more "hip" in it as it goes along.* **ROSETTA**, *for her part, is even more exuberant in her delivery than before.*)

YOU HOLD ME IN YOUR BOSOM
TILL THE STORMS OF LIFE IS OVER
RRRRRRRRRROCK ME
IN THE CRADLE OF OUR LOVE
ONLY FEED ME TILL I WANT NO MORE
THEN YOU TAKE ME TO YOUR BLESSED HOME ABOVE

MAKE MY JOURNEY BRIGHTER

YOU MAKE MY BURDEN LIGHTER
HELP ME TO DO GOOD WHEREVER I CAN
OH, LET THOU PRAISE AND THRILL ME
THOU LOVING KINDNESS FILL ME
THEN YOU HOLD ME
HOLD ME IN THE HOLLOW OF YOUR HAND

YOU HIDE ME IN YOUR BOSOM
TILL THE STORMS OF LIFE IS OVER
RRRRRRRRROCK ME
IN THE CRADLE OF OUR LOVE
ONLY FEEEEEEEEEED
THEN YOU'LL TAKE ME TO YOUR BLESSED HOME ABOVE

(The song finishes. It was good, but the air in the room is still a bit chilly. Into the silence:)

MARIE. Was that
Was that more what you –?

ROSETTA. Just about just about

MARIE. Sister
I'm sorry I –

ROSETTA. No
You forgiven
We all forgiven
Seven times seventy
You remember that Madame Marie
Whatever foolish nonsense we get into down here
Whatever ROCK ME's that sound a little too one way or another
We all forgiven in the end

(MARIE nods.)

I know swingin' it may seem strange but
"Sing to the Lord a new song"
That's what the Good Book say
A new song
That's all we doin'
Singin' a new song

(**MARIE** *nods.*)

ROSETTA. So?
Think you can get there?

MARIE. I'll put my mind to it

ROSETTA. Your mind?

MARIE. *(Smiling.)* My hips
It still don't feel natural but I –
How'd you learn it?

ROSETTA. Shoot
Born with it
Six years old
Playing in front of the congregation
Standing on top of the piano so people could see me
Even then my hips couldn't keep from swingin'
Too much swing for a small town

MARIE. I'll bet

ROSETTA. Mother Bell never paid them no mind though
All the tsk tsk-ers
Mother Bell was proper church but she knew if she clamped down on my hips she'd be messing with my metronome
So she took my hips outta Arkansas instead
Moved us to Chicago
Saturday night she'd preach outside the Bronzeville bars till they closed
Sunday morning I'd sing for the service
Just the two of us in the big ole city
'Scuse me
Three of us

(**ROSETTA** *walks across the room.*)

MARIE. Three?

ROSETTA. Time for you to meet my right hand

(**ROSETTA** *opens a guitar case and takes out a huge acoustic guitar.*)

MARIE. Oh but I'm only just

ROSETTA. No it's time

Now that we got that piano of yours loosened up a little

MARIE. Could we do another one without it first

ROSETTA. Sorry Little Sister

Wandalyn's putting on her lips

You wanted to get used to me right?

You gotta get used to all'a me

[MUSIC NO. 05 "SIT DOWN"]

(**ROSETTA** *plays a chord or riff on her guitar.*)

MARIE. Yes but

I'm not sure how to play with that

How I'm s'posed to play with the way you play it

ROSETTA. Well Little Sister you better find out

(**ROSETTA** *launches into "Sit Down." She plays an unexpectedly mean guitar, and belts the song out for all it's worth.*)

WHY DON'T YOU SIT DOWN?
I CAN'T SIT DOWN
SIT DOWN I TOLD YOU
I CAN'T SIT DOWN
GO AWAY DON'T BOTHER ME
I CAN'T SIT DOWN
BECAUSE I JUST GOT TO HEAVEN AND I CAN'T SIT DOWN

(*Guitar solo.*)

WHO'S THAT YONDER DRESSED IN WHITE?
I JUST GOT TO HEAVEN AND I CAN'T SIT DOWN
IT LOOKS LIKE THE CHILDREN OF THE ISRAELITE
I JUST GOT TO HEAVEN AND I CAN'T SIT DOWN

(*Guitar solo, then on the next verse* **MARIE** *tentatively finds her way into accompanying* **ROSETTA**. *She's getting there.*)

ROSETTA.

WHO'S THAT YONDER DRESSED IN RED?
I JUST GOT TO HEAVEN AND I CAN'T SIT DOWN

IT LOOKS LIKE THE CHILDREN THAT MOSES LED
I JUST GOT TO HEAVEN AND I CAN'T SIT DOWN
    (Guitar solo.)
WHY DON'T YOU SIT DOWN?
I CAN'T SIT DOWN
NO NO NO NO NO NO
I CAN'T SIT DOWN
GO AWAY DON'T BOTHER ME
I CAN'T SIT DOWN
BECAUSE I JUST GOT TO HEAVEN AND I CAN'T SIT DOWN

SIT DOWN I TOLD YOU
I CAN'T SIT DOWN
MMM MMM NO
I CAN'T SIT DOWN
THEN GO AWAY DON'T BOTHER ME
I CAN'T SIT DOWN
BECAUSE I JUST GOT TO HEAVEN AND I CAN'T SIT DOWN

SIT DOWN
NO NO NO NO NO
I CAN'T SIT DOWN
NO NO NO NO NO NO NO
I CAN'T SIT DOWN
BECAUSE I JUST GOT TO HEAVEN AND I CAN'T SIT DOWN
    (Guitar solo.)
WHY DON'T YOU SIT DOWN?
NO I CAN'T SIT DOWN
GO AWAY DON'T BOTHER ME
I CAN'T SIT DOWN
UH UH
I CAN'T SIT DOWN
BECAUSE I JUST GOT TO HEAVEN AND I CAN'T SIT DOWN!

    (**ROSETTA** *erupts with joy.*)

That's it Little Sister!

Little Sister finding her hips!

MARIE. You think so?

ROSETTA. Now's the fun part

Now we put it all together
You fine on piano but you know I didn't pick you for that

MARIE. No

ROSETTA. You know I didn't take you away from your husband and children for no piano

MARIE. No

ROSETTA. Time to *sing* Little Sister
Both of us

MARIE. All right

ROSETTA. How those hands?

MARIE. Trembling

ROSETTA. Good
A tremble is close cousin to a swing
How 'bout "Didn't it Rain"?
That churchy enough for you Madame Marie?

MARIE. All right

ROSETTA. Then hang on

[MUSIC NO. 06 "DIDN'T IT RAIN"]

(**ROSETTA** *launches into "Didn't it Rain," an upbeat, joyful tune.* **MARIE** *is a little looser.*)

TELL ME DIDN'T IT RAIN RAIN RAIN CHILDREN
RAIN OH MY LORD

(**ROSETTA** *stops cold,* **MARIE** *follows.*)

MARIE. Was that not –?

ROSETTA. Piano was fine
You not singing

MARIE. You didn't get to the chorus yet

ROSETTA. The chorus?
No
No no no no no no no
You not waiting till the chorus little girl
You on

When I'm on you on

MARIE. What do you mean?

ROSETTA. You ain't in the Sunset Four no more honey

MARIE. I know but

ROSETTA. I know what you used to

Harmonizing with those three other girls choirmaster drilled it into your head don't showboat don't be louder than them other girls

MARIE. That's right

ROSETTA. Well forget all that

MARIE. Forget it?

ROSETTA. You not my back-up Little Sister
You my "and"

MARIE. Your what?

ROSETTA. My "and"
Sister Rosetta Tharpe *and* Marie Knight

MARIE. Really?

ROSETTA. Really
So you give it to me, you hear?

MARIE. All of it?

ROSETTA. You give me everything you got

(**MARIE** *nods, nervous, but now having the time of her life. They launch back into "Didn't It Rain." This time it's all there, the harmonies, the call and response, the piano and guitar. It's joyful, glorious.*)

TELL ME

BOTH.
DIDN'T IT RAIN RAIN RAIN
CHILDREN RAIN OH MY LORD

MARIE.
DIDN'T IT

ROSETTA.
YES

MARIE.
>DIDN'T IT

ROSETTA.
>YOU KNOW IT DID

MARIE.
>DIDN'T IT

BOTH.
>OH OH MY LORD DIDN'T IT RAIN
>TELL ME
>DIDN'T IT RAIN RAIN RAIN
>CHILDREN RAIN OH MY LORD

MARIE.
>DIDN'T IT

ROSETTA.
>YES

MARIE.
>DIDN'T IT

ROSETTA.
>YOU KNOW IT DID

MARIE.
>DIDN'T IT

BOTH.
>OH OH MY LORD DIDN'T IT RAIN

>>(**ROSETTA** *gestures for* **MARIE** *to take lead.*)

MARIE.
>WELL IT RAINED FORTY DAYS
>IT RAINED FORTY NIGHTS
>THERE WAS NO LAND NOWHERE IN SIGHT
>GOD SEND THE RAVEN TO BRING THE NEWS
>HE HOIST HIS WINGS AND AWAY HE FLEW
>JUST SING IT

ROSETTA.	**MARIE.**
I SAID IT RAINED	I MEAN IT
YOU KNOW IT RAINED	IN THE EAST
OH HOW IT RAINED	AND IN THE WEST
IT RAINED TOO LONG	IN THE NORTH

MY IT RAINED
RAIN ALL DAY
RAIN ALL NIGHT
RAIN RAIN
BLIND RAIN
MMM RAIN
RAIN RAIN RAIN RAIN
   RAIN RAIN
RAIN RAIN RAIN RAIN

AND IN THE SOUTH
ALL DAY
AND ALL NIGHT
AND ALL NIGHT
AND ALL DAY
WELLLLLLL

TELL ME DIDN'T IT

BOTH.
   RAIN RAIN RAIN CHILDREN
   RAIN OH MY LORD
MARIE.
   DIDN'T IT
ROSETTA.
   YES
MARIE.
   DIDN'T IT
ROSETTA.
   YOU KNOW IT DID
MARIE.
   DIDN'T IT
BOTH.
   OH OH MY LORD DIDN'T IT RAIN
   TELL ME
   DIDN'T IT RAIN RAIN RAIN
   CHILDREN RAIN OH MY LORD
MARIE.
   DIDN'T IT
ROSETTA.
   YES
MARIE.
   DIDN'T IT
ROSETTA.
   YOU KNOW IT DID

MARIE.
>DIDN'T IT

ROSETTA.
>OH OH MY LORD DIDN'T IT RAIN

MARIE.
>WELL IT RAINED FORTY DAYS
>FORTY NIGHTS WITHOUT STOPPING
>NOAH WAS GLAD WHEN THE WATER STOPPED DROPPING
>WHEN I GET TO HEAVEN I'LL SIT RIGHT DOWN
>ASK KING JESUS AND HIS STARRY CROWN

ROSETTA.	**MARIE.**
I KNOW IT RAINED	YES IT DID
I'M TIRED OF IT RAININ'	I MEAN IT
IT'S RAININ' TOO LONG	IN THE EAST
A RAIN ALL DAY	AND IN THE WEST
ALL NIGHT LONG	IN THE NORTH
A RAIN RAIN GO AWAY	AND IN THE SOUTH
COME AGAIN SOME OTHER DAY	ALL DAY
YOU KNOW IT RAINED	AND ALL NIGHT
OH HOW IT RAINED	AND ALL NIGHT
GOD KNOWS IT RAINED	AND ALL DAY
RAIN RAIN RAIN RAIN RAIN RAIN RAIN RAIN	WELLLLLLL

MARIE.
>TELL ME
>DIDN'T IT

BOTH.
>RAIN RAIN RAIN RAIN CHILDREN
>RAIN OH MY LORD

MARIE.
>DIDN'T IT

ROSETTA.
>YES

MARIE.
>DIDN'T IT

ROSETTA.
>YOU KNOW IT DID

MARIE.
>DIDN'T IT

BOTH.
>OH OH MY LORD DIDN'T IT RAIN!

>>*(They end the song with a flourish.* **ROSETTA** *applauds, explodes.)*

ROSETTA. Ooo! Ooo!
>We gettin' there!
>Now we gettin' there!
>Lord let me catch my breath

MARIE. It was good?

ROSETTA. Don't play the shy violet with me baby
>You know you done good
>Jesus is happy and so am I
>I knew we was gonna sound like somethin' I knew it
>Ooo Mahalia's gonna be mad
>She didn't know what she nearly got

MARIE. You really want me to
>To sing all-out like that

ROSETTA. That's right
>I ain't made a' china I ain't gonna break
>Aw world better get ready for us
>Good and ready
>Rosetta and Marie

MARIE. Yeah

ROSETTA. Say it I wanna hear you say it

MARIE. Rosetta and Marie

ROSETTA. Again

MARIE. Rosetta and Marie

ROSETTA. Again

MARIE. Rosetta and Marie

ROSETTA. That's right

You keep that up and 'fore too long it's gonna be Marie
and Rosetta
MARIE. *(Blushing.)* No
ROSETTA. Once they get a look at you
At your pretty little thing up there
Two babies huh?
MARIE. That's right
ROSETTA. Mercy you kept your figure
MARIE. No
ROSETTA. You kept it something fierce
MARIE. You too
ROSETTA. Oh I kept it all right
I kept it growing
MARIE. No
ROSETTA. But thanks anyway
Thanks for picking up your cue

> *(Pats her belly.)*

Lord
I don't even have a baby excuse
It's the road
You'll see
You eat whatever the driver can rustle up
Gospel chicken and sweet tea
Then you get out there and sing
And when you finish you ready to eat all over again
MARIE. Gospel chicken?
ROSETTA. Bologna
Restaurants won't give black folk nothin' hot
MARIE. Don't think I like bologna
ROSETTA. You will
MARIE. Not tonight
(Of the funeral home.) I won't gain an ounce in here
Won't be able to eat no gospel chicken with ghosts
around

ROSETTA. Good

Good

Then we'll book nothing but funeral homes from now on

Keep you nice and trim

>   *(She looks* **MARIE** *over.)*

Oh Lord

I know I'm gonna lose the mens

I'll lose the mens the minute you walk on stage

MARIE. Sister that's nice of you and all but nobody's gonna be looking at me

ROSETTA. How you figure that?

MARIE. Once you start playing that guitar I'm gone

ROSETTA. Naw

MARIE. Once you start pickin' I'm gonna fade away

ROSETTA. No no

MARIE. Like one of these ghosts

ROSETTA. Well

All right then well maybe

You may flicker in and out now and then

Hard not to look at me when my guitar gets to testifyin'

But backstage?

Can bet those bookers'll be lookin' at you

You might throw 'em a smile or two

Make sure they don't cheat us none

Maybe even get us a better cut

How you at countin'?

MARIE. Countin'?

Beats?

ROSETTA. Maths

MARIE. Maths I'm good

ROSETTA. Good

That's you

That'll be you too

MARIE. What?

ROSETTA. Takin' care of all that money
   Who gets what
   What cut goes where
   I can't be bothered with all that
   I'll sleep in a casket
   Set up my tone box myself
   Push the piano onstage
   But a diva has her limits

MARIE. You trust me with that?
   Already?

ROSETTA. More than any'a my husbands that's for sure
   A bunch'a squirrels
   Squirrelin' away my money for a rainy day
   If Foch ever shows up you tell him to squirrel somewhere else
   Tell him you in charge of the wallet now

MARIE. Foch your husband?

ROSETTA. Sorta
   But clock's tickin' on that one
   They gonna be an "ex" in front of that "husband" soon enough
   Lord Lord
   Another one cut loose

MARIE. Goodness
   Say
   How...

      *(**MARIE** turns silent, serious.)*

   How do you do that?
   Get that "ex"?

ROSETTA. Ooo Little Sister got a squirrel of her own

MARIE. I do

ROSETTA. That husband I didn't know about about to become someone I don't need to know

Well
I'm sorry Little Sister
Hard to believe someone wouldn't know what they had with you
Must be soft in the head
He soft in the head?

MARIE. No
He's a preacher

ROSETTA. Oh honey you tell me that's not true

MARIE. I ain't lyin'

ROSETTA. Lord a preacher
They the worst squirrels they is
You watch
Every church we play on this tour
Every preacher gonna whisper in your ear
You think a little swing is sin
You listen to some of that whisperin'
Oh but I know I know how it goes with you
I had me a preacher man

MARIE. You did?

ROSETTA. Sure
Squirrel number one
We'd travel all over Illinois in a beat-up Ford
Had us an act
He'd preach and I'd sing

MARIE. That's what we did too
All 'round New Jersey

ROSETTA. Oh Little Sister
Poor Little Sister
They change don't they
Even the preachers
'Specially the preachers
They start out all right that's what gets you every time they start out fine but they change

MARIE. That's it
>All he ever wanted when we started out was to hear me sing
>Sing him to sleep every night
>Sing him awake
>Then
>So fast
>Blink and it got so he'd shush me every time I opened my mouth
>Didn't want to hear a note
>"Shush Marie
>Shush"
>Got so sick of my voice he up and walked out on me
>Left me and the kids to fend for ourselves
>I don't know what happened

ROSETTA. I think it's the sharin' that does it
>Havin' to share you with the world
>Your gift
>It makes 'em proud at first but then
>Then
>Turns out they not so good at sharin'

MARIE. Maybe so

ROSETTA. I can share honey
>You'll see
>That spotlight gonna be shinin' on both of us
>You don't need no squirrel
>Time for that squirrel to go

MARIE. But ain't that a sin
>I vowed to be his forever

ROSETTA. He the one that broke the vow Little Sister not you
>You free to go

MARIE. But a preacher

ROSETTA. A preacher's harder to get rid of yeah but I done it

You just go to court and you "yes" that judge right into a divorce
"Did he treat you bad?"
"Yes"
"Did he abandon you?"
"Yes"
A few more a those and then that's that
Cry a little for the icing
Maybe tell them he hit you

MARIE. But he didn't
Did yours?

ROSETTA. Sure
In the kitchen
Out in the middle of the street
For talkin' back
For forgettin' to wear a hat
I put up with it
Longer than I should've
Part of me felt like that was the price maybe
Price for all'a that applause
Smack on the head to keep it outta the clouds

MARIE. What made you finally…?

ROSETTA. Clobbered me so hard one night it left a ringing in my ears
Picked up my guitar and couldn't hear a couple'a the high notes through the ringing
Squirrel wasn't just messing with me now
He was messing with my music
A few hours later the ringing faded away and so did I
Left Squirrel flat
I said to myself that man can mess with a lot of things
But he will not mess with my music
I grabbed Mother Bell and we were off to New York
I even gave myself a middle name for a while
"Vashti"

MARIE. From the Bible?
ROSETTA. That's right
Mmm-hm
Queen Vashti who refuses to obey her king
Sister Rosetta Vashti Tharpe
I'll give myself as many damn –
(To **MARIE.***)* Pardon
(To the Heavens.) Pardon
– Names as I please
MARIE. *(Amazed.)* You just left
ROSETTA. Yep
MARIE. Just went to court and
ROSETTA. Simple as that
Is he messing with your music?
MARIE. Yes
ROSETTA. Then it's as simple as that
Tell you what
I'll go with you
MARIE. Really?
ROSETTA. Better yet I'll testify myself
I'll get rid of mine you get rid of yours
Double date
MARIE. All right
ROSETTA. First thing when we get back to New York

(**ROSETTA** *looks at* **MARIE** *admiringly.*)

Lord
I wish Mother Bell could see what I found
MARIE. She pass?
ROSETTA. Recent
Sing one for her?
So she can meet you?
MARIE. Hip?
ROSETTA. No
No hip

[MUSIC NO. 07 "CALL MY NAME IN PRAYER"]

(MARIE *starts the song on piano,* ROSETTA *listening deeply.*)

MARIE.
>WHILE KNEELING BY HER BEDSIDE IN A COTTAGE ON THE HILL
>MY MOTHER PRAYED HER BLESSINGS ON ME THERE
>SHE WAS TALKING THERE TO JESUS WHILE EVERYTHING WAS STILL
>AND I HEARD MY MOTHER CALL MY NAME IN PRAYER
>
>YES, I HEARD MY MOTHER CALL MY NAME IN PRAYER
>SHE WAS POURING OUT HER HEART TO JESUS THERE
>THEN I GAVE MY HEART TO HIM AND HE SAVED MY SOUL FROM SIN
>FOR HE HEARD MY MOTHER CALL MY NAME IN PRAYER
>
>SHE WAS ANXIOUS FOR HER GIRL TO BE JUST WHAT SHE OUGHT TO BE
>AND SHE ASKED THE LORD TO TAKE HER IN HIS CARE
>NOW JUST THE WORDS THE WORDS I CAN'T REMEMBER BUT I KNOW SHE PRAYED FOR ME
>FOR I HEARD MY MOTHER CALL MY NAME IN PRAYER

>(ROSETTA *joins, quietly.*)

BOTH.
>YES, I HEARD MY MOTHER CALL MY NAME IN PRAYER
>SHE WAS POURING OUT HER HEART TO JESUS THERE
>THEN I GAVE MY HEART TO HIM AND HE SAVED MY SOUL FROM SIN
>FOR HE HEARD MY MOTHER CALL MY NAME IN PRAYER

>(*Quiet.*)

ROSETTA. Thank you

MARIE. 'Course
>Don't know what I'd do without mine

ROSETTA. I won't lie
>It's hard

Mother Bell stood by me chaperoned me my whole life
Now...

MARIE. "Lift the stone and you shall find her
Split the wood and she is there."

   (**ROSETTA** *nods, grateful for the comfort.*)

ROSETTA. Amen
Amen
And you
I know you a good mother too
I can tell

   (**MARIE** *darkens, guilt descending.*)

MARIE. Don't feel like one now
Off halfway round the world

ROSETTA. You providin' that's all

MARIE. Still
Leaving is leaving
Never left them alone for more than a night

ROSETTA. They not alone
Your mama'll take good care'a them

MARIE. She'll do her best
But it's not the same

ROSETTA. No
No kids'a my own but I can imagine
Look at it this way
Your mama raised you and you turned out just fine
She'll do the same for them

MARIE. Yes but she
She won't tuck them in right
They love how I tuck them in

ROSETTA. Sure

MARIE. When they're finally spent after another tornado day
Drained

Too tired to fend off my hugs and kisses now
And secretly not wanting to
Wanting me to kiss them into their dreams
My mama got a terrible voice
Just terrible
Who's singing them to sleep?
ROSETTA. God is
He's humming a lullaby as they lay down they heads
MARIE. Yes but
My kids're
They're not a couple'a squirrels I want to get rid of
I miss them already
I think I'm gonna miss them too much
ROSETTA. Tour won't last forever child
MARIE. I know but
No 'fense but
You don't know how they change
How every second they become something else and what they were is gone
I'm gonna miss all those seconds
They're gonna be different when I get back
ROSETTA. So will you
You'll be comin' back a star
Your light blinding bright
MARIE. Still
ROSETTA. We'll ask Walter if you can use the telephone later
Call home
Talk to your babies
My dime

(A moment.)

Listen
You got to choose
God gave you this gift
You got to choose what to do with it

Rock and a hard place:
Either
You roll down the Gospel Highway
See how bright your light can shine
Send money back to the children you never see

MARIE. Or?

ROSETTA. Or stay at home
Sing on Sundays for a grateful congregation
Kiss your babies goodnight
Rest of the week be a maid at best

[MUSIC NO. 08 "THIS TRAIN"]

(MARIE heads to the piano. She riffs around, then starts to sing. The first verse is on the melancholy side, but she grows increasingly raucous with each verse thereafter.)

MARIE.
THIS TRAIN'S NO PLACE FOR BABIES, THIS TRAIN
THIS TRAIN'S NO PLACE FOR BABIES, THIS TRAIN
THIS TRAIN'S NO PLACE FOR BABIES
NO IFS, NO ANDS, NO BUTS, NO MAYBES
THIS TRAIN'S NO PLACE FOR BABIES, THIS TRAIN

BUT THIS TRAIN DON'T HAUL NO SQUIRRELS, THIS TRAIN
THIS TRAIN DON'T HAUL NO SQUIRRELS, THIS TRAIN
THIS TRAIN DON'T HAUL NO SQUIRRELS
DON'T CARRY NOTHING BUT GIRLS WITH PEARLS
THIS TRAIN DON'T HAUL NO SQUIRRELS, THIS TRAIN

'CAUSE THIS TRAIN'S FOR ROSETTA AND MARIE, THIS TRAIN
THIS TRAIN'S FOR ROSETTA AND MARIE, THIS TRAIN
THIS TRAIN'S FOR ROSETTA AND MARIE
SAVE YOUR SOUL, YOU WAIT AND SEE
THIS TRAIN'S FOR ROSETTA AND MARIE, THIS TRAIN

(The two share a laugh. A moment as ROSETTA stares at MARIE, lost in her beauty.)

ROSETTA. God you pretty

MARIE. No

ROSETTA. God did a number on you
    You pretty enough to stop Time
    You know you made Kermit skip a beat

MARIE. What?

ROSETTA. Last night
    He was moonlighting with Mahalia's band and once he got a good look at you he kinda shivered and he up and missed a beat
    You know he closed his eyes the rest of the song
    Only way he could keep Time in hand

MARIE. *(Blushing once more.)* Now

ROSETTA. Poor little beat
    Lost forever
    Where'd it go you think?

MARIE. I don't know

ROSETTA. Drifted off into the Heavens unstruck
    Or down into an unmarked grave
    Or maybe it didn't go nowhere
    Maybe it stayed in Kermit
    Maybe drummer beat's gotta stay with him
    Maybe went up to his head made it sore
    Maybe an extra beat of his heart
    Or maybe it went somewhere lower
    Knowing Kermit that's probably it
    Thump
    Thump and he smiled at me like a cat in his cream
    Thump

MARIE. *(Protesting, but a bit weakly.)* This talk
    It's a sin

ROSETTA. No
    I stare at you long enough to know I'm being a fool but anything less and I'm a bigger one
    God sends me this face and I look away?

That would be the sin
That would be the sin

> *(A moment between them.* **MARIE** *smiles, conspiratorially.)*

MARIE. Let's

ROSETTA. What?

MARIE. Could we try

[MUSIC NO. 08A "BEFORE TALL SKINNY PAPA"]

> *(She plays a riff on the piano.)*

ROSETTA. How you know that one?

MARIE. Um
Daddy had the record

ROSETTA. Figures
Musta everybody's daddy had that record
Still livin' it down

MARIE. He hid it away in the sleeve of another one
I thought it seemed too thick and out come two records 'stead of one
I put it on real quiet while Mama was doing dishes
Almost lost my mind
Was that really you?
With that big ole band?

ROSETTA. Yeah
Damn –
(To **MARIE.***)* Pardon
(To Heaven.) Pardon
– Cotton Club contract
Had to sing any fool thing they put in front of me

MARIE. I practiced it

ROSETTA. What do you mean?

MARIE. On the piano

ROSETTA. In the church?

MARIE. (*Blushing.*) Yes

ROSETTA. Oh Lord

MARIE. Every day after class
>Sang along real quiet
>Turned around one day and there's the Sunday school teacher standing right behind me ruler ready in her hand

ROSETTA. Oh honey

MARIE. She worked my knuckles till they bled

ROSETTA. They bled
>And you still wanna play it?

MARIE. Even now makes 'em ache
>But yes
>With you right in front of me no record at all but alive yes

ROSETTA. All right
>Wandalyn can wait a minute
>But you gotta sing too

MARIE. I will

>(**ROSETTA** *puts her guitar in her case.*)

ROSETTA. No guitar on this one
>Gotta keep that pure
>Keep it for the Lord

>(**MARIE** *nods and starts. After a few measures,* **ROSETTA** *signals her to stop.*)

>Hold up

MARIE. What?

>(**ROSETTA** *closes the lid on the guitar case, locks it up.*)

ROSETTA. Can't be too careful

[MUSIC NO. 09 "TALL SKINNY PAPA"]

>(**MARIE** *nods and starts again, launching into the song. Her piano has picked up a considerable amount of raunch.*)

I WANT A TALL SKINNY PAPA
MARIE.
YEAH!
ROSETTA.
I WANT A TALL SKINNY PAPA
MARIE.
YEAH!
ROSETTA.
I WANT A TALL SKINNY PAPA
MARIE.
YEAH!
ROSETTA.
I WANT A TALL SKINNY PAPA
MARIE.
YEAH!
ROSETTA.
I WANT A TALL SKINNY PAPA
THAT'S ALL I'LL EVER NEED
MARIE.
SHE WANTS A TALL, TALL, TALL SKINNY PAPA
TALL, TALL, TALL SKINNY PAPA
TALL, TALL, TALL SKINNY PAPA
TALL, TALL, TALL SKINNY PAPA
ROSETTA.
I WANT A TALL SKINNY PAPA
THAT'S ALL I'LL EVER NEED

HE'S GOT TO BE ALL MINE
TREAT ME FINE
WALK THE CHALK LINE
AND STAY ON MY MIND
HE'S GOT TO BE ALL RIGHT
LEARN TO FIGHT ALL NIGHT
MAMA WILL DO THE REST
NOW HOW 'BOUT THAT MESS?
HE'S GOT TO DO WHAT HE'S TOLD
AND BRING SWEET MAMA THAT GOLD
TO SATISFY MY SOUL

MARIE.
>HE'S GOTTA BE A TALL, TALL, TALL SKINNY PAPA

BOTH.
>TALL, TALL, TALL SKINNY PAPA
>TALL, TALL, TALL SKINNY PAPA
>TALL, TALL, TALL

MARIE.
>SKINNY PAPA

ROSETTA.
>I WANT A TALL SKINNY SQUIRREL

BOTH.
>THAT'S ALL I'LL EVER NEED
>>*(They finish, laughing.)*

ROSETTA. So your knuckles hurt?

MARIE. They do they do

ROSETTA. Then we must be doin' it right

>*(**ROSETTA**, having fun, joins **MARIE** on the piano bench.)*

Shoot as long as I put the guitar away:

[MUSIC NO. 10 "FOUR FIVE TIMES"]

>*(**ROSETTA** plays, **MARIE** joining in, four hands on deck.)*

FOUR OR FIVE TIMES
FOUR OR FIVE TIMES
IT'S MY DELIGHT
DOING THINGS RIGHT
FOUR OR FIVE TIMES

NOW MAYBE I'LL SIGH
AND MAYBE I'LL CRY
BUT IF I DIE
I'M GONNA TRY TO DO IT
FOUR OR FIVE TIMES
I SAID FOUR OR FIVE TIMES

MARIE.
>FOUR OR FIVE TIMES

ROSETTA.
>OH, FOUR OR FIVE TIMES

MARIE.
>FOUR OR FIVE TIMES

ROSETTA.
>NOW HE'S MY KING
>HE MAKES ME SWING
>FOUR OR FIVE TIMES
>
>I CONFESS

MARIE.
>I CONFESS

ROSETTA.
>HE'S THE BEST

MARIE.
>HE'S THE BEST

ROSETTA.
>HE PASS THE TEST
>KILL THAT MESS
>FOUR OR FIVE TIMES

MARIE.
>FOUR OR FIVE TIMES

ROSETTA.
>FOUR OR FIVE TIMES

MARIE.
>FOUR OR FIVE TIMES

ROSETTA.
>OH, FOUR OR FIVE TIMES

MARIE.
>IT'S MY DESIRE
>TO SET THE WORLD ON FIRE
>FOUR OR FIVE TIMES
>AND MAYBE I'M WRONG

ROSETTA.
>MAYBE I'M WRONG

MARIE.
>OR MAYBE I'M RIGHT

ROSETTA.
>MAYBE I'M RIGHT

MARIE.
>BUT RIGHT OR WRONG
>I'M GONNA SWING THIS SONG
>FOUR OR FIVE TIMES

>>(**MARIE** *and* **ROSETTA** *trade off solos.*)

ROSETTA.
>I SAID FOUR OR FIVE TIMES

MARIE.
>FOUR OR FIVE TIMES

ROSETTA.
>FOUR OR FIVE TIMES

MARIE.
>FOUR OR FIVE TIMES

ROSETTA.
>IT'S MIGHTY NICE
>DOING THINGS RIGHT
>FOUR OR FIVE TIMES
>NOW MAYBE I'LL SIGH

MARIE.
>MAYBE I'LL SIGH

ROSETTA.
>AND MAYBE I'LL CRY

MARIE.
>MAYBE I'LL CRY

ROSETTA.
>BUT IF I DIE
>I'M GONNA TRY TO DO IT
>FOUR OR FIVE TIMES
>ONE

MARIE.
>TWO

ROSETTA.
>THREE

MARIE.
>FOUR

BOTH.
>AH FOUR OR FIVE TIMES!
>>*(Big finish.)*

ROSETTA. Now we both going to Hell

MARIE. What's that like
>Singing in a club?

>*(**ROSETTA** opens up her case, gets her guitar out.)*

ROSETTA. See that's what Saint Mahalia don't understand
>Says she'll only sing in church
>But tell me if I'm wrong:
>I'm gonna find more sinners in a nightclub than she ever gonna find in a church

MARIE. Sing it

ROSETTA. Plus
>Got to play with Duke Ellington Cab Calloway Hot Lips Page
>You may go looking but you ain't gonna find them playin' for the Sunday service
>I was there though
>Every Sunday
>I'd play church in the morning Cotton Club that night
>Brought a little club into the church and a little church into the club

>*(A cloud over **ROSETTA**'s face.)*

>Does cross your mind though
>Standing in front of a plantation backdrop
>Singin' those silly songs
>You can dress as proper as you like
>Tell yourself you're doing God's work
>But when you got half-naked dancing girls brushing up against you
>When you playin' clubs your friends can't set foot in
>Putting on blackface for the Saint and Sinner acts
>Playing the dumb Holy Roller for a laugh

Staring out at all those smiling and drinking white faces
Sometimes it makes you wonder if it ain't pennies from Heaven all over again

[MUSIC NO. 11 "I LOOKED DOWN THE LINE"]

(**ROSETTA** *plays deep blues quietly, to herself more than to* **MARIE**.)

WELL I LOOKED DOWN THE LINE AND I WONDERED
AND I WONDERED
AND I WONDERED
I LOOKED DOWN THE LINE AND I WONDERED
JUST TO SEE HOW FAR THAT I WAS FROM GOD

OH THE LINE LOOKED SO SAD AND LONESOME
SAD AND LONESOME
SAD AND LONESOME
THE LINE LOOKED SO SAD AND LONESOME
JUST TO SEE HOW FAR THAT I WAS FROM GOD

THEN I BUCKLED UP MY SHOES AND I STARTED
AND I STARTED
GOD KNOWS THAT I STARTED
I JUST BUCKLED UP MY SHOES AND I STARTED
JUST TO SEE HOW FAR THAT I WAS FROM GOD

MMM
MMM
MMM
MMM
MMM MMM

THEN I LOOKED IN THE GRAVE AND I WONDERED
AND I WONDERED
AND I WONDERED
I LOOKED IN THE GRAVE AND I WONDERED
JUST TO SEE HOW FAR THAT I WAS FROM GOD

OH THE GRAVE LOOKED SO SAD AND LONESOME
SAD AND LONESOME
SAD AND LONESOME

THE GRAVE LOOKED SO SAD AND LONESOME
JUST TO SEE HOW FAR THAT I WAS FROM GOD

> (**ROSETTA** *finishes, seems a bit overcome.*
> **MARIE** *takes her hand.*)

MARIE. Seven times seventy

ROSETTA. Seven times seventy
It's a wondrous thing
That kinda love
Hard to wrap your head round
Hard to wrap it round but easy to sing about

> (**ROSETTA** *is a little lost;* **MARIE** *stears her back with:*)

MARIE. We done them all?

ROSETTA. Hm?

MARIE. The songs, Wandalyn's rounding the corner

ROSETTA. Right no we still got a couple more
Big Finish

> (*A secret smile flits across* **ROSETTA**'s *face.*)

And I got something special to push us over

> (**ROSETTA** *walks across the room.*)

Something I been waiting to try out in front of a crowd

> (**ROSETTA** *opens a guitar case and pulls out a shiny white guitar.*)

MARIE. It's beautiful

ROSETTA. It's heavy
Here

> (**ROSETTA** *hands the guitar to* **MARIE**.)

MARIE. Oh my goodness
Why's it so heavy?

> (**ROSETTA** *lifts her finger to tell* **MARIE** *to wait and pulls out a small amplifier. She takes the guitar back from* **MARIE** *and dangles the guitar chord suggestively.*)

ROSETTA. Well?

Plug me in and you'll find out

> (**MARIE** *does so. There is a crackle and she jumps back.*)

MARIE. That isn't –

> (**ROSETTA** *strums a chord. It is loud, really loud.*)

Is that –

That's an electric?

> (**ROSETTA** *nods and plays "yes."*)

You got an electric?

> (**ROSETTA** *nods and plays "yes."*)

Play it play it

> (**ROSETTA** *knocks out a solo, wailing and with reverb, a kid with a new toy. She ends with a flourish.*)

Oh gracious

You were worried about church folk before

ROSETTA. Naw c'mon now

'Lectricity nothin' new

Church folk not living with candles anymore

They'll just have to get used to it

> (*She strums a power chord that lasts forever.*)

I'm gonna be a lady Gabriel

A big ole fat loud as get-out lady Joshua

> (**ROSETTA** *plays another power chord.*)

You think you can play with us tonight?

MARIE. I don't see why not

"Beams of Heaven"?

ROSETTA. No

New guitar new song

Let's make us up a new song I hear music in the air

[MUSIC NO. 12 "UP ABOVE MY HEAD"]

(ROSETTA noodles around on the guitar, searching for a melody. She finds one; MARIE joins with piano. ROSETTA starts to hum along, finding a vocal melody. MARIE joins her in the humming. ROSETTA tries out a lyric in a call and response and MARIE answers. We watch the song come together before our eyes, a creation from the two of them, theirs.)

ROSETTA.
UP ABOVE MY HEAD
MARIE.
UP ABOVE MY HEAD
ROSETTA.
I HEAR MUSIC IN THE AIR
MARIE.
I HEAR MUSIC IN THE AIR
ROSETTA.
NOW UP ABOVE MY HEAD
MARIE.
UP ABOVE MY HEAD
ROSETTA.
YOU KNOW I HEAR MUSIC IN THE AIR
MARIE.
I HEAR MUSIC IN THE AIR
ROSETTA.
UP ABOVE MY HEAD
MARIE.
UP ABOVE MY HEAD
ROSETTA.
I HEAR MUSIC IN THE AIR
MARIE.
I HEAR MUSIC IN THE AIR
ROSETTA.
AND I... I REALLY DO BELIEVE

MARIE.
>YES! I REALLY DO BELIEVE

ROSETTA.
>THERE IS A HEAVEN SOMEWHERE

BOTH.
>HEAVEN SOMEWHERE

>>*(They launch into the song at full tempo.)*

ROSETTA.
>UP ABOVE MY HEAD

MARIE.
>UP ABOVE MY HEAD

ROSETTA.
>I SEE TROUBLE IN THE AIR

MARIE.
>I SEE TROUBLE IN THE AIR

ROSETTA.
>UP ABOVE MY HEAD

MARIE.
>UP ABOVE MY HEAD

ROSETTA.
>I SEE TROUBLE IN THE AIR

MARIE.
>I SEE TROUBLE IN THE AIR

ROSETTA.
>UP ABOVE MY HEAD HEAD HEAD

MARIE.
>UP ABOVE MY HEAD

ROSETTA.	**MARIE.**
I SEE TROUBLE IN THE AIR, OH, AND	I SEE TROUBLE IN THE AIR

BOTH.
>I REALLY DO BELIEVE

ROSETTA.
>YES!

BOTH.
>I REALLY DO BELIEVE

THERE'S A HEAVEN SOMEWHERE
ROSETTA.
HEAVEN SOMEWHERE
MARIE.
ALL IN MY HOME
ROSETTA.
ALL IN MY HOME
MARIE.
I HEAR MUSIC IN THE AIR
ROSETTA.
I HEAR MUSIC IN THE AIR
BOTH.
ALL IN MY HEART
MARIE.
I HEAR MUSIC IN THE AIR
ROSETTA.
I HEAR MUSIC IN THE AIR
MARIE.
ALL IN MY HOME
ROSETTA.
HOME, WHOA
MARIE.
I HEAR MUSIC IN THE AIR, MUSIC IN THE AIR
BOTH.
AND I REALLY DO BELIEVE
ROSETTA.
YES!
BOTH.
I REALLY DO BELIEVE
THERE'S A HEAVEN SOMEWHERE
ROSETTA.
HEAVEN SOMEWHERE

>   (**ROSETTA** *solos, loud and proud on the electric guitar.*)

ROSETTA.
UP ABOVE MY HEAD

MARIE.
UP ABOVE MY HEAD
ROSETTA.
I HEAR MUSIC IN THE AIR
MARIE.
I HEAR MUSIC IN THE AIR
ROSETTA.
I SAID UP ABOVE MY HEAD
MARIE.
UP ABOVE MY HEAD
ROSETTA.
I HEAR MUSIC IN THE AIR
MARIE.
I HEAR MUSIC IN THE AIR
ROSETTA.
UP ABOVE MY HEAD HEAD HEAD
MARIE.
UP ABOVE MY HEAD
ROSETTA.
I HEAR MUSIC IN THE AIR OH YES AND
MARIE.
I HEAR MUSIC IN THE AIR
BOTH.
I REALLY DO BELIEVE
I REALLY DO BELIEVE
THERE'S A HEAVEN SOMEWHERE
HEAVEN SOMEWHERE.

> *(They stare at each other, their perfect and powerful harmony hanging in the air.)*

ROSETTA. There's heaven all right
There's heaven right here
MARIE. It's like it's all my voice
All one voice
ROSETTA. Amen
Marie?

MARIE. Yes

ROSETTA. This is gonna work
>I know this is gonna work now
>I don't need tonight to figure it out
>This is gonna work

MARIE. I think so too

ROSETTA. And I want you to stick around but I have to ask you somethin'
>As good as we sound
>As good as this could be
>If there's still part of you that doubts me
>Doubts my faith
>I can't have you be one of those tsk-tskers
>Can't invite a tsk-tsker up on stage with me
>To sing with me every night
>Into that holy space
>That communion space
>Do you understand?

MARIE. I do

ROSETTA. So you tell me now if you going to look down on me in some secret place in your heart
>Cuz if that's true
>Good as you sound
>Pretty as you look
>Precious as you are
>I got to let you go

>### [MUSIC NO. 12A "AMAZING GRACE #2"]

>*(A moment. Then **MARIE** plays, first straight, then after a moment, swinging the notes as far as they will bend. **ROSETTA** beams. **MARIE** raises her hand to signal a joke while continuing to play with the other:)*

MARIE. Oh and Sister
>I'm gonna need a microphone

You're playing that thing

> *(The electric guitar.)*

I'm gonna need to be louder

> (**ROSETTA** *laughs.*)

ROSETTA. Oh you sure gonna be fun after all girl
Thank God Almighty you gonna be fun

MARIE. So
You warmed up enough for this one yet?

[MUSIC NO. 13 "STRANGE THINGS"]

> *(With that,* **MARIE** *segues into the intro to "Strange Things Happen Every Day".* **ROSETTA** *smiles, nods. She picks up her electric guitar and joins* **MARIE***'s piano. They move into the song proper, the performance a conversation between the two, a revival, a love affair, a binding of spirits.)*

ROSETTA.
OH, WE HEAR CHURCH PEOPLE SAY
THEY ARE IN THE HOLY WAY
THERE ARE STRANGE THINGS HAPPENING EVERY DAY
ON THAT LAST GREAT JUDGEMENT DAY
WHEN THEY DRIVE THEM ALL AWAY
THERE ARE STRANGE THINGS HAPPENING EVERY DAY

EVERY DAY

MARIE.
EVERY DAY

ROSETTA.
EVERY DAY

MARIE.
EVERY DAY

ROSETTA.
THERE ARE STRANGE THINGS HAPPENING EVERY DAY

MARIE.
EVERY DAY

ROSETTA.

EVERY DAY
MARIE.
EVERY DAY
ROSETTA.
EVERY DAY
THERE ARE STRANGE THINGS HAPPENING EVERY DAY
MARIE.
JESUS IS THE HOLY LIGHT
TURNING DARKNESS INTO LIGHT
THERE ARE STRANGE THINGS HAPPENING EVERY
DAY
OH, HE GAVE THE BLIND MAN SIGHT
AND HE PRAISED HIM WITH ALL HIS MIGHT
THERE ARE STRANGE THINGS HAPPENING EVERY DAY

> (**ROSETTA** and **MARIE** trade solos back and forth, playing at their loosest and loudest, showing off for each other. They close with:)

ROSETTA.
IF YOU WANT TO VIEW THE CLIMB
YOU MUST LEARN TO QUIT YOUR LYIN'
THERE ARE STRANGE THINGS HAPPENING EVERY DAY
IF YOU HEAR RIGHT THROUGH THE LIES
YOU CAN LIVE RIGHT ALL THE TIME
THERE ARE STRANGE THINGS HAPPENING EVERY DAY
OH, EVERY DAY
MARIE.
EVERY DAY
ROSETTA.
OH, EVERY DAY
MARIE.
EVERY DAY
ROSETTA.
WHOA THERE ARE STRANGE THINGS HAPPENING EVERY
DAY
MARIE.
EVERY DAY

ROSETTA.
>OH, EVERY DAY

MARIE.
>EVERY DAY

ROSETTA.
>OH, EVERY DAY, OH

BOTH.
>THERE ARE STRANGE THINGS HAPPENING EVERY DAY.

>>(**MARIE** *applauds.*)

ROSETTA. You save some of that for yourself now

>>(**MARIE** *won't stop applauding, delirious with joy.*)

Cut it out you making *me* blush

>>(**MARIE** *stops, but is no less excited, continues:*)

MARIE. We close with that right?

ROSETTA. Don't have a bigger one

MARIE. That one's big enough
Big enough for Johnny Cash
His favorite song
Big enough for Little Richard
Etta James
Jimi Hendrix
Big enough for Elvis too
You're his favorite guitar player you know
Told Scotty "play it like Rosetta"
Drove Scotty crazy
"Play it like Rosetta
Play it like Rosetta"

>>(**MARIE** *doesn't notice that* **ROSETTA** *isn't laughing, she is looking* **MARIE** *over with suspicion.*)

ROSETTA. Who's that?

MARIE. Who?

ROSETTA. Elvis?

MARIE. Elvis

You know Elvis

ROSETTA. I most surely don't

And Jimi who?

MARIE. Hendrix

>(**MARIE** *stops short.*)

He

He's

>(*A shift.*)

ROSETTA. Strange things

This

MARIE. Let's just try that one again –

ROSETTA. This is a strange thing isn't it Little Sister?

MARIE. Rosetta we got a show to –

ROSETTA. No

No we don't

Do we?

This isn't Walter's

>(*A moment.* **MARIE** *is truly cornered now, and strangely seems to almost age before us. The lights shift, turn colder.*)

MARIE. ...No

ROSETTA. Ain't Mississippi either

Too cold for Mississippi

MARIE. Philadelphia

ROSETTA. Philadelphia what am I doing in...

MARIE. It's where

Where you end up

ROSETTA. Where I –?

>(**ROSETTA** *looks around her at the coffins, the funeral home, and the truth dawns.*)

Oh

Oh

MARIE. I couldn't help myself
    I came in here and I started touching up your face and I couldn't help my mind from thinking
    Going back
    That first night
    Just the two of us putting together our show
    Well
    That's just about the best night of my life

ROSETTA. Mine too Little Sister
    Mine too
    So you know don't you
    You know everything after Walter's
    What happens next

MARIE. I do

ROSETTA. Tell me
    The gig that night
    Was I right?
    All those Wandalyns like us?

MARIE. They love us

ROSETTA. And the next night?
    The next?

MARIE. Thousands of people a night
    Thousands of dollars a week
    Fur coats
    Mink stoles
    In New York City we have to hire an ambulance to get us from the Downtown gigs to the Uptown ones in time
    Touching up each other's faces in the back of an ambulance
    Running every red light in Manhattan
    Sister you were right
    You make me a star

ROSETTA. Good

Then what?
We get rid of our squirrels?

MARIE. We do
You buy a new house
>   *(Blushing.)*

For us
You me my kids
One happy family

ROSETTA. I can see it
I can see it clear
It last forever?
Tell me we last forever

>   (**MARIE** *says nothing.*)

Marie?

MARIE. Three years

ROSETTA. Three?
That's all?

MARIE. It was a telephone call
A call for me in the middle of one of our tours

ROSETTA. Who?
A record company?

MARIE. No

ROSETTA. Mahalia
It was Mahalia

MARIE. No
Just a neighbor
A woman who did washing for the block
She called to tell me there'd been a fire
Fire at my mama's place while we were gone

ROSETTA. No
No

MARIE. While Mama was minding the kids

ROSETTA. No honey

MARIE. That they'd all
ROSETTA. Not your babies
MARIE. My mama my babies all of them
ROSETTA. Little Sister
MARIE. Had to bury my people one day come back and play Des Moines the next
ROSETTA. Sister
MARIE. Broke me for a while
Broke Time too
Finally stopped It from moving so fast
Each hour without them a lifetime
Crawling my way through Time to get to the end of the day
ROSETTA. You shoulda let me take care of you
MARIE. You tried
Hard as you could
But it was time for me to go
Back to the church for me
Oh Rosetta
You won't believe it
Became a preacher
Preacher of my very own church
ROSETTA. I wish I could hear you sermonizin'
MARIE. You do
You did
ROSETTA. Good
I don't become no preacher
MARIE. No
You keep on playing
Get married again
Squirrel number three
In a baseball stadium
ROSETTA. A baseball stadium?
MARIE. Twenty-five thousand people show up
More people than were at the game that afternoon

Every one of them bringing a wedding present
You say your vows then kiss the groom then strap on that guitar in your white gown and heels and the crowd goes crazy

ROSETTA. Twenty-five thousand

MARIE. Yes

ROSETTA. And then...

> (**MARIE** *can't continue.*)

Truth

MARIE. ...They're gone
They vanish just like that
You become an oldies act overnight
Play a stadium one year church basement the next
You get a bruise on your leg
Won't go away grows
Turns out it's the sugar the gout
You lose it
Squirrel Three sticks you out there anyway wants that money
You hoppin' around on one leg playing guitar
Even one leg wasn't gonna stop you from putting on a show
But guess you can only hop around so long
So
So you wind up here

ROSETTA. Philadelphia

MARIE. I take the first plane
Push that undertaker aside
Wipe off the dime store junk he's put on your face
Start over
Make you over
Like I used to
More of a challenge now
Sugar that took your leg paled your face
But I do it

    I make that face over till you're as beautiful as you ever were
    Put you in your best dress
    Put your favorite guitar in your hands
    Something to keep you company

ROSETTA. Thank you

MARIE. I just wish…

    (**MARIE** *breaks down.* **ROSETTA** *reaches out to* **MARIE,** *concerned.*)

ROSETTA. Honey stop that

MARIE. It's not right
    I don't have the money to
    An unmarked grave
    For you?
    It ain't right
    No one remembering your name

ROSETTA. You'll remember
    And God
    God will
    And every time He think of that silly girl playing that guitar He'll chuckle and smile
    Here

    (**ROSETTA** *holds out her guitar to* **MARIE.**)

    What you gonna sing?
    You can't tell me you not gonna sing something at the service

    (**MARIE** *smiles, takes the guitar.*)

MARIE. They couldn't stop me

ROSETTA. I know that
    You gonna close it out aren't you?

MARIE. Yes

ROSETTA. Well?

MARIE. Well?

ROSETTA. Well let's hear it

MARIE. Now?

ROSETTA. You need to practice, right?
   Ain't this where we practice?

MARIE. Yes
   Yes it is
   It may...
   It may tremble though
   Not my hands this time
   My
   And not 'cause of nerves
   You'll forgive me if it trembles

ROSETTA. Honey
   Little Sister
   I'll forgive you anything

   [MUSIC NO. 14 "PEACE IN THE VALLEY"]

   (**MARIE** *strums the guitar, admires it, then sings. Her voice trembles with emotion here and there, but she triumphs over it and sings magnificently.*)

MARIE.
   I'M TIRED AND WEARY, BUT I MUST TRAVEL ON
   TILL THE LORD COMES AND CALLS ME AWAY
   WHERE THE MORNING'S SO BRIGHT AND THE LAMB IS
      THE LIGHT
   AND THE NIGHT IS AS BRIGHT AS THE DAY

   THERE'LL BE PEACE IN THE VALLEY FOR ME SOME DAY
   THERE'LL BE PEACE IN THE VALLEY FOR ME OH LORD I
      PRAY
   THERE'LL BE NO SADNESS, NO SORROW, NO TROUBLE I
      SEE
   ONLY PEACE IN THE VALLEY FOR ME
   WELL THE BEAR WILL BE GENTLE AND THE WOLVES WILL
      BE TAME
   AND THE LION SHALL LAY DOWN WITH THE LAMB OH YES
   AND THE BEASTS FROM THE WILD SHALL BE LED BY A
      CHILD

AND I'LL BE CHANGED FROM THIS CREATURE I AM
YES, THERE WILL BE PEACE IN THE VALLEY FOR ME SOMEDAY
THERE'LL BE PEACE IN THE VALLEY FOR ME I PRAY
THERE'LL BE NO SADNESS, NO SORROW, NO TROUBLE I SEE
ONLY PEACE IN THE VALLEY FOR ME

> *(Quiet. They sit for a moment, gaze at each other.)*

ROSETTA. Marie...

MARIE. ...I know

> *(A moment between them, then:)*

It's time
You hold on to this now
Tight

> *(**MARIE** hands **ROSETTA** back her white guitar.)*

ROSETTA. My scar?

> *(**MARIE** looks **ROSETTA** over.)*

MARIE. Still covered up

ROSETTA. My blush?

MARIE. Still looks good
Just one more thing

> *(**MARIE** takes out a tube of lipstick. She tries to place it on **ROSETTA**'s lips, but her hand trembles too much. Finally, she places it on her own lips and then kisses **ROSETTA**. She looks over her handiwork.)*

Now
Now you're ready to sing

> *(Lights fade out.)*

End of Play

www.ingramcontent.com/pod-product-compliance
Ingram Content Group UK Ltd.
Pitfield, Milton Keynes, MK11 3LW, UK
UKHW022041160625
459754UK00004B/25

9 780573 706417